A journey *with* friends

EXPLORING COMMUNITY

A journey *with* friends

EXPLORING COMMUNITY

Kate Hayes

A journey with friends: exploring community

An individual or small group Bible resource from Scripture Union

Scripture Union, 207-209 Queensway, Bletchley, MK2 2EB, England, UK
Email: info@scriptureunion.org.uk
Website: www.scriptureunion.org.uk

ISBN: 978 1 84427 357 7

Scripture Union Australia
Locked Bag 2, Central Coast Business Centre, NSW 2252
www.su.org.au

First published in the UK by Scripture Union, 2008

Scripture taken from the New Living Translation, British text, published by Tyndale House Publishers, Inc., Wheaton, Illinois, USA, and distributed by STL Ltd., Carlisle, Cumbria, England.

British Library Cataloguing-in-Publication data
A catalogue record for this book is available from the British Library.

Cover design: Philip Grundy

Internal design and typesetting by Servis Filmsetting Ltd, Stockport, Cheshire

Printed in Singapore by Tien Wah Press

☙ Scripture Union is an international Christian charity working with churches in more than 130 countries, providing resources to bring the good news about Jesus Christ to children, young people and families and to encourage them to develop spiritually through the Bible and prayer.
As well as our network of volunteers, staff and associates who run holidays, church-based events and school Christian groups, we produce a wide range of publications and support those who use our resources through training programmes.

The Way Ahead

*D*o you sometimes find people annoying, demanding or plain impossible to get along with? Perhaps after a bad few days you find yourself daydreaming of a retreat on a desert island or in a mountain refuge and spending time in peace and quiet, alone. Getting along with people is rarely easy, but for those who have chosen to follow Jesus abandoning human contact is not an option. We are called to live life alongside others, to take part in God's purposes for the world as his church, together. Our relationships with our fellow believers help to mould us into the kind of people God wants us to be.

In this series we look at Paul's letter to the Philippian church. They weren't a church full of perfect people, but they did have a desire to follow Jesus, and Paul encourages them to see that this is best done in partnership with others. Paul doesn't pretend that such a call is easy, but he reminds us that in Jesus we have both the model for our relationships and our way of life. Not only that, he points out that our ability to live like Jesus is not dependent solely on our own efforts which can so often let us down. Instead we can rely on the power of Jesus to work in us. It is Jesus himself who enables us to live lives that bring honour to his name.

We are also reminded that we are called to live God's way for a reason. It's not just for our own benefit that God wants us to take a risk and rebuild a broken relationship, to persevere when we are discouraged or to learn how to trust God for our present and our future. As followers of Jesus there is a bigger picture, a bigger purpose to life. We are called to shine his light into the world around us, to point others to him. The way we live our lives day by day is the way we can demonstrate the truth of God's power to change lives, make a difference to the world we live in and help others to experience that life-changing love for themselves.

This book will suit those who read it alone and also those who are taking part in regular meetings with a small group. Sometimes there are suggestions for activities that are particularly suitable for someone to do alone or in a group and those are indicated with the following logos.

The Solitary Traveller

This book is a companion for the solitary traveller. You can work through the material at your own pace, ignoring only those sections marked with the group logo. It may be helpful for you to record your thoughts along the way, either on the pages or in a separate notebook.

The Group of Travellers

This book is also a companion for the small group. You may have come together with a Christian friend, as a prayer triplet, as an existing small fellowship group or you may be part of a group specially convened for Lent or some other season of the year. Decide whether one person will lead each time you meet, or whether a different person will lead each session. Some may want to skip those sections marked with the solitary traveller logo but it is also possible to use these sections within the group by allowing people time for silent reflection.

Using the Material

The material is divided into six sessions or chapters and there is a consistent pattern to the material in each.

Setting Out will ease you gently into the focus of the session through some fun questions or activities. Don't skip this part, even if you are reading the book alone, because however light this material seems it will flag up some important attitudes and preconceptions and will prepare you for deeper exploration of some key issues. Within the group setting, this opening time will develop relationships and encourage honest sharing which will ultimately help the group to be more comfortable together.

Signposts will take you into the Bible. This time of discovery is designed to open up a number of lines of thought as you follow through the questions. For groups, this section will particularly encourage discussion and the sharing of experiences.

Prayer is the next section, during which time there is opportunity to pray in a way that relates to the focus of the session so far. Don't be tempted to rush this; it is just as important as the rest of the session.

Finally, there is a **Further Afield** section. This allows you further exploration of related issues in the Bible. Depending on how long you have together, groups wanting to lengthen the Bible study section could use some or all of this material in the **Signposts** section. Otherwise group members might like to use **Further Afield** at home for personal study during the week. Individuals can choose to use some or all of this section.

1   *Take it or leave it*

Going it alone can seem very tempting when everyone around you is falling out or when you're working with the incompetent, lazy or just plain irritating. Whilst there are many times we can cut free from others and strike out on our own, that option isn't really given to us as God's people. We are called to live life together. Everyone's gifts are necessary to fulfil God's purposes and we need strong relationships to help us keep on track. Here we see how the relationship between Paul and the Philippians has much to teach us about working together.

Setting Out

Who was your best friend when you were at primary school? What was it that made you good friends? Did it last, are you still in touch today?

Many friendships begin through a shared interest or experience of some kind. Perhaps you've worked on a project together, gone to the same Weight Watchers group or found a hobby in common. Have you made friendships through experiences like these?

Shared experience doesn't guarantee friendship, does it? Have you always been good friends with everyone in your class at school or with all your work colleagues? Why is that?

Is it possible to work well with people you aren't friendly with, perhaps even don't like? What makes that so?

Signposts

CALLED TO PLAY A PART

Read Philippians 1:1–7

We've probably all belonged to something at one time or another, perhaps a branch of the Guides or Scouts, a sports club or a singing group. What are some of the groups you've been part of? What are you a member of today?

Being a member of something doesn't automatically lead to involvement. Gyms make a lot of money out of people who sign up in a fit of enthusiasm but then never go along. Others join an organisation such as the National Trust but never visit their properties and don't get involved with their campaigns. Have you ever been a member of something and ended up making little or no use of that membership? Why was that?

On the whole membership allows us to decide just how much of a commitment we make to that group or organisation. It's usually perfectly possible to join and do nothing else afterwards. However, maybe describing ourselves as a member isn't always helpful. When you thought about your memberships, did you include your church?

People often do see themselves as members of a particular church. It's possible that such an attitude can mean it becomes like being a part of any other group, something we choose to get involved with, or not, as it suits us.

Do you think that is true? If so, does it matter?

Instead of speaking about the Philippians as church members, Paul uses a very different phrase (1:5). Paul describes them as 'partners in spreading the Good News'.

What do you think are the differences between being a member of a church and a partner in it?

What about your church? Do you think most people see themselves as members or partners? What makes you say that?

How might we encourage Christians who are reluctant to share in service and ministry to get involved as partners in the gospel?

OUR NEED FOR OTHERS

Paul was a great ambassador for Jesus. He even described himself as an example for others to follow (Philippians 3:17), not because he was perfect, but because he knew he was wholehearted in following Jesus. If anyone was strong enough to serve Jesus without any support from others, then surely Paul was that man. However, even Paul looked out for people who would be his partners, people who would work with him for the sake of the gospel.

Why do you think it was so important for Paul to have partners in his ministry?

Partnership didn't necessarily mean being physically alongside Paul as he worked. How did the Philippians partner Paul?

SUCCESSFUL PARTNERSHIPS

Being a follower of Jesus is about more than the state of our private walk with God. We are called into partnership in God's work; called to serve him together. Successful partnerships are built on three shared elements, elements demonstrated in Paul's partnership with the Philippians.

1 SHARED PURPOSE (1:5)

What task were Paul and the Philippians both committed to?

That shared sense of purpose and direction meant the relationship between Paul and the Philippians was more than that of teacher and pupils, guide and followers. They were working together to achieve God's purposes.

2 SHARED PRESENCE (1:6)

Their relationship was also built on the presence of God at work in them all.

Paul says that it is God who initiates his good work in us. Do you think God reaches out to everyone at some time or another? If so, why do some of us respond and not others?

Have you ever ignored God reaching out to you? Why was that?

God doesn't just reach out to us and then abandon us once we've responded to him. Paul says God continues his work in us right up to the final day. When you look back can you see key moments in your life when God was at work? Perhaps you can remember a time when God brought you back from the brink, taught you something new or demonstrated his power in your life. You might like to share these things with one another.

We are all a work in progress, none of us is perfect, and we rely on God's power to work in us and change us. How could that truth strengthen our relationships with one another?

3 SHARED COMMITMENT (1:7 AND PHILIPPIANS 1:28,29)

Imagine you have planned to spend a free day doing some much needed decorating when a good friend rings up and suggests you go out for the day together. Do you

- fling your brushes away without a thought and get ready;
- go into overdrive and do a high-speed half-hearted job in one hour flat;
- go out and then stay up half the night doing the painting;
- suggest that if your friend wants to see you, they could come and help you paint;
- ring work and book another day off to do the painting next week instead;
- tell them you just can't meet them today, perhaps another time?

Even if you would have stayed focused here, are there other situations where you are easily distracted?

When Paul wrote this letter he was in prison far away from the Philippians who were themselves facing opposition and suffering. The continued spread of the Good News was under threat. However, they didn't allow these things to distract them from the task in hand; their sense of purpose remained undimmed.

Working alongside one another in partnership built the relationship between Paul and the Philippians into one marked by love, joy and encouragement. Involvement in God's work brought them hard challenges but also this great depth of relationship as well. By sharing together in ministry we too can find this deeper sense of community.

TO CONSIDER

Have you ever found that working alongside someone in ministry deepened your relationship with them?

Are you involved in some kind of service or ministry yourself?
If so, who do you share that ministry with?

Are these relationships marked by the shared purpose, presence and
commitment seen between Paul and the Philippians?
If the answer isn't 'yes, all the time', what particular area could you work on?

Not only shared ministry can lead to these kinds of relationships.
A small group can build relationships on these same three foundations too.
Even shared commitment doesn't have to mean we are all passionate about the
same things, but that we are all passionate to see God at work in our lives, our
church and our community.

How can a small group be a source of joy and encouragement to those in it?

What part can you play in this?

Prayer

Paul's warm feelings for the Philippians aren't just feelings, they result in
action, not least in time spent praying for them regularly. Do we pray for all
those whose lives are significant to us, those we live with, work with, serve
with and do life with?

Paul's prayer shows us how to do this. You may want to reread **Philippians
1:9–11.** (Perhaps try *The Message* translation.)

Paul prays the Philippians will have

1. Love

Paul isn't praying for warm, gushy feelings towards one another or towards God.
What characterises the love he prays for?

2. Understanding

The NLT translates the beginning of v 10 as 'understand what really matters'.

What does 'really matter'? What does Paul want the Philippians to be able to do?

3. Finally, *The Message* translation of v 10b speaks about 'living . . . a life Jesus will be proud of'.

What makes our lives something Jesus will be proud of?

Make a list of some key people you serve with and share life with. If you are meeting with a group then don't forget them too.

Think back to Paul's prayer for the Philippians (1:9–11) and use it as a guide as you spend a few minutes praying silently for some of those on your list.

End by using Paul's words as a prayer for one another. You may like to read them aloud together, or if the group isn't too big, use the words to pray for each person in turn, adding their name at the beginning.

I pray that your love will overflow more and more, and that you will keep on growing in knowledge and understanding. For I want you to understand what really matters, so that you may live pure and blameless lives until the day of Christ's return. May you always be filled with the fruit of your salvation – the righteous character produced in your life by Jesus Christ – for this will bring much glory and praise to God.

Further Afield

1 GOD'S POWER TO CHANGE LIVES

Read Acts 7:57–8:3 and Acts 9:1–20

Do you know people who seem very far away from entering into a relationship with Jesus?

Sometimes we can pray for people for many years and yet they still seem just as far away from God. Saul, the leading persecutor of the church, wasn't promising Christian material. It seems probable that the Christians of that time prayed not just that Saul would stop but that he would come to know Jesus for himself. Eventually God managed to communicate with Saul in a way that convinced him that Jesus was alive and real.

Why do you think God used such a dramatic method of communicating with Saul?

Why do you think he doesn't speak to us all in this way?

What brought the members of your group to know Jesus for the first time? Most people don't meet Jesus through miraculous events but through friendship and the ordinary events of life. Eventually something happens that makes the person willing to give God a chance.

Pray for those known to you who don't follow Jesus. Pray that something would make them willing to give God a chance. Be ready to play a part in that if necessary.

2 INVEST IN RELATIONSHIPS

Imagine you've been given a free day; there's no compulsion to do anything. Would you spend it relaxing alone or with friends or would you choose to spend it catching up on household tasks or other jobs? Some of us are people who find it hard to sit down and relax, others take every opportunity to do so! What about Paul, how does he strike you? Do you imagine him taking time out to relax?

Sometimes we can see Paul as so intensely sold out for God that he seems intimidating and hard to know.

Read Acts 20:36–21:1; 28:15 and 1 Thessalonians 2:17

In these verses we see tears on Paul's departure, people walking thirty or forty miles to meet him on his arrival in Rome and his longing to see friends. These aren't the experiences of a man who was difficult to be with but of one who invested a great deal of time and energy into his relationships with his brothers and sisters.

If Paul could make the time to build relationships with those he taught and served alongside, so can we. Maybe you could put aside some extra time this week to spend with others. If that's not possible, maybe you could use the time you are already spending with someone and make an extra effort to build up that relationship.

3 SWEETNESS AND LIGHT

Read I Peter 4:8 and Proverbs 27:17

Some people like to keep their relationships warm and easy at all times, happy to overlook problems and potential disagreements. Others are willing to say what they think and raise problems in their relationships if necessary. Which of these is most like you?

Which attitude do you prefer to find in those around you? Why?

Obviously there is a difference between being contentious for the sake of it and raising important issues, just as there is a difference between being peace-loving and brushing things under the carpet. True friendship, the kind that Paul sought and that we should be willing to build with our brothers and sisters in Christ, is two things:

1. Slow to get angry, willing to overlook most failings in the other person (1 Peter 4:8)

2. Ready to raise issues when it's really important (Proverbs 27:17)

Who amongst your circle of friends is willing to do both those things for you?

Are you able to do them for others?

What do you think are the benefits of running our relationships according to these two principles?

Pray that God will give you the wisdom to apply these two principles to your relationships.

Ask him to show you if there is someone you need to show more patience with and grace to, or someone you need to be more honest with from now on.

2 How to cope with hard times

Jesus says we will experience trials and sorrows (John 16:33) and we all know that is true. Knowing that difficulties are inevitable, we can choose to sit back and hope we cope, or we can try to prepare ourselves for what lies ahead. Paul experienced many difficulties from beatings to shipwreck, and the way he dealt with them offers us guidance we can follow in our own lives.

Setting Out

Things aren't going well and you've taken a day off work because you desperately need a break. Suddenly there's a knock at the door and a good friend is standing there. Would you most like them to:

- suggest you go out for the day to do something you both enjoy: shopping, walking, going out to eat, going to the gym. . .;
- come in and listen patiently to you sounding off about life, the universe and everything;
- offer a small gift and an encouraging card and then go away and leave you in peace;
- come in and make themselves useful doing those boring chores that are getting you down: the ironing, mowing the lawn, the minor repairs . . .;
- ignore the fact that things are bad in your life and pour out their own problems to you?

Why would you find that most helpful?

What would you have found least helpful?

Which do you think you would be most likely to offer to a friend of yours in need? Or would you do something else?

When things are difficult in your life do you find it easy to ask others for help or not? Why?

Signposts

DEALING WITH DISASTER

Read Philippians 1:12–26

Paul is under house arrest — unable to travel and teach as he wants. To anyone looking on things weren't going too well. Not only was Paul personally restricted, it seemed that the cause of the Gospel was also at risk.

How might you have expected Paul to feel under these circumstances?

When you read the passage, how do you think he really is feeling about his imprisonment?

Imagine you were trying to describe Paul's personality and character to another person. What would you say about him?

We see Paul's response to his difficulties and perhaps we almost believe him to be completely different from ordinary people like you and me. We wonder if he was some kind of superman, someone almost untouched and untroubled by hardship, someone who could endure these things beyond anything we could ever expect to emulate. However, that wasn't really the case.

Read 2 Corinthians 7:5–7

How did Paul feel on his arrival in Macedonia?

What changed that?

This is just one example of a time when Paul did feel afraid and discouraged. In reality Paul was no more a superman than you or I are. How Paul differed from most of us was not in his feelings but in his response to the difficult situations he found himself in. Here as he faces a frustrating imprisonment and the threat of death, we can learn what helped him deal with difficulty in such a positive way.

1 HE TRUSTED GOD HAD NOT FORGOTTEN HIM

Sometimes when people are going through a hard time they believe God has
abandoned them, that he doesn't care about them. Have you ever
experienced this happening to you?

How can we encourage someone when they are feeling like this?

Read Luke 12:6,7

Jesus reminds us that God never forgets us or stops caring for us. Paul may well
have felt abandoned at times, but he didn't allow those feelings to overwhelm
him; neither did he grit his teeth and blindly hope these words were true.
Instead of getting trapped by feelings he chose to look for evidence of God's
continuing presence with him.

What evidence did Paul have that God was still at work in his life?
(Philippians 1:12)

Paul's imprisonment gave him opportunities to share the gospel with his jailers
and to encourage others. Do you think that good things resulting from his
imprisonment meant God wanted it to happen?

'It's for your own good.' Has anybody ever said that to you? Have you ever been
unhappy about doing something and yet known that in the end it was the
best thing for you?

In Romans 8:28 Paul says, 'And we know that God causes everything to work
together for the good of those who love God and are called according to his
purpose for them'.

Paul doesn't say that God promises to make us happy. So what does he mean by
saying things will work out for our good?

Paul does not deny the truth that we face many situations that are very difficult
to deal with. He doesn't say we can't be sad or angry or frustrated by them and
he doesn't mean that every bad experience is deliberately thrown at us by God.
Instead he reminds us that in the midst of our darkest and most shattering
experiences God is still with us, using them to bring us closer to him and make
us more like Jesus.

Have you experienced God bringing good out of difficult times in your life?

How different things would have been if Paul had believed that difficult circumstances meant that God had abandoned him. Sometimes we'll be faced with situations that mean we have to change the way we serve God, maybe even give up something altogether for a time. Even so God is still at work in us and we are never forgotten.

2 HE DIDN'T GO IT ALONE

Imagine you've been unavoidably detained far away from everyone you really care about. You can't go to them and if they are to come to you it will be a long, possibly dangerous and time-consuming trip. There are no phones, no email, no Skype, MSN or Facebook and the ordinary mail is slow and unreliable. Would it matter to you being so isolated? Why?

When life is tough, how does that affect your relationship with God and his people? Do you

- spend more or less time alone with God;
- go to church more or less often;
- spend more or less time with other Christians?

Why is that?

Paul was no loner; he did mind being separated from others. When later he was imprisoned for the final time, he appealed to Timothy to come quickly as 'only Luke is with me' (2 Timothy 4:9–12). Then in verse 16 he continues, 'The first time I was brought before the judge, no one was with me. Everyone had abandoned me'. Like us Paul felt lonely and found the support of others helped him face up to the many challenges in his life.

The Philippians were a great encouragement to Paul. We've already seen they encouraged him through their continuing faith and partnership with him (Philippians 1:3–7). Here we see another key element in their support: upholding him before God (Philippians 1:19)

The Philippians couldn't directly solve Paul's problems; they couldn't pull strings and bring about his release. What they did do is pray for him.

Sometimes we may know people in difficulty, perhaps they're very ill or caught up in apparently insoluble situations and we commit to praying for them. However, even though we know God is all powerful we still may not always feel able to pray for complete healing or a perfect resolution to their problems. Should we still pray for them?

Apart from a perfect resolution, how else can we pray for people who are struggling?

For Paul to be encouraged by the Philippians' prayers, they had to tell him about them.

Do you tell people when you are praying for them?

Why might we pray for someone and not tell them we are doing it?

How does it, or would it, make you feel if someone told you they were praying for you?

Is there ever a downside to telling someone you are praying for them?

The Philippians' prayers told Paul he was not facing this situation alone. They were aware of what was happening to him and were holding him up before God.

Do you know people that need your prayers to uphold them through a tough time? Have you told them you are praying for them? If not, why is that? How do you think they would feel if you did tell them?

3 HE WANTED TO BRING HONOUR TO JESUS (1:20–22)

100 best films to see before you die. . . 100 things to do . . . 100 classic books to read, places to go, mountains to climb, even best bridges to visit! There are innumerable lists of bests to experience before we die. The implication is that we don't want to miss out on the great experiences of life, nor waste precious time on lesser things.

If you'd been told you would die, which of these lists would you most like to have the chance to work through?

Most of these lists are going to take a while to complete and are probably composed by people who really aren't expecting to die anytime soon. Paul is facing the possibility of death and isn't concerned about the experiences he's missing out on. What does matter to him?

Sometimes our attitude to death suggests the things we have in life are more precious than what lies ahead. Paul's view is very different. He says, 'For to me living is for Christ and dying is even better' (v 21).

Does Paul's view that dying is the best outcome mean he is unhappy or doesn't care about those close to him?

Whatever happened to him, Paul was committed to living a life that honoured Jesus. For Paul, life was a precious gift but it was temporary, a first step to something even better.

How do you think such an attitude affected Paul's actions?

Do you see your life as a first step to a future with Jesus?

How do you think such an attitude should affect the way we behave day by day?

Paul looked beyond his circumstances to trust in God's enduring love and faithfulness. Such attitudes didn't spring fully-formed just when he realised he might die. Instead, they were learnt by practising them again and again in the face of many smaller challenges. One day we too may need the same faith and hope Paul had. Emulating Paul's example means practising those attitudes now day by day.

TO CONSIDER

Do you allow circumstances to influence your trust in God? Do you act as if God loves you more in the good times than in the bad?

How do you respond to difficulty?
- Do you look out for signs of God at work in your life?
- Do you share your problems with others?
- Do you allow them to encourage and support you?
- Do you keep your eyes focused on Jesus no matter what?
- Do you believe that, whatever happens, God is with you?
- Do you know that certainty of life beyond death that brings hope in every situation?

What could you do differently next time life throws you a challenge of this kind?

Prayer

Struggling people may find it hard to pray and spend time with God. One way to support them is to take responsibility and uphold them before God.

Spend a few moments thinking of people who need your prayers and support at the moment and then take time to pray for them.

You may like to go round the group, each inserting a name to complete the prayer 'Lord we uphold (NAME) before you. Comfort and strengthen them today', or the group may wish to pray their own short prayers for the people they are concerned about. However, be wary of gossiping; be careful not to reveal confidential details of their problems under the guise of praying for them.

There may also be members of the group facing difficult challenges. Offer them a chance to share their concerns, in whatever depth they choose and then pray for them too.

End by saying these words of David:

'The Lord is my rock, my fortress, and my saviour; my God is my rock, in whom I find protection. He is my shield, the strength of my salvation, and my stronghold, my high tower, my saviour, the one who saves me from violence. I will call on the Lord, who is worthy of praise, for he saves me from my enemies.

The waves of death surrounded me; the floods of destruction swept over me. The grave wrapped its ropes around me; death itself stared me in the face. But in my distress I cried out to the Lord; yes, I called to my God for help. He heard me from his sanctuary; my cry reached his ears.

O Lord, you are my light; yes, Lord, you light up my darkness. In your strength I can crush an army; with my God I can scale any wall.'

2 Samuel 22:2b–7; 29–30

Further Afield

1 TAKING A BACK SEAT

Read Philippians 1:12

Paul's role in spreading the good news has changed. Instead of being out in the front line planting new churches he is forced to take a back seat.

How do you think Paul felt about being compelled to stop doing the work he loved?

Why did the continuing faith and ministry of the Philippians encourage Paul in his imprisonment?

Have you ever been forced by circumstances to take a back seat in an area of ministry you had given a great deal of time and energy to? If so, how did it make you feel?

Changing roles can be difficult. We may look at what God is doing without our involvement and feel jealous, sidelined or frustrated, maybe even bitter. Here Paul chooses to focus not on what he can't do, but on what God is still doing. God's purposes are still being fulfilled; the good news is still being shared.

Pray for any you know who have had to take a step back from ministry, perhaps due to their health, for example. Do you know how they are coping with those changes? How could you encourage them this week?

2 TAKING OUR OPPORTUNITIES

Did you get into trouble a lot at school? What did your school do about children who misbehaved?

In punishing someone there is the hope they won't do it again and perhaps also a warning to others not to follow suit. In imprisoning Paul the authorities probably hoped others might be more reluctant to speak about Jesus themselves.

Read Philippians 1:12–18

If you knew that somebody had been imprisoned for speaking about Jesus, would that make you more or less likely to do the same yourself?

Paul says his imprisonment encouraged the local Christians to speak more boldly about Jesus than before. Why do you think that was?

Pray for Christians who face imprisonment for speaking about Jesus. Pray that like Paul they would remain bold in the face of that threat. Paul was encouraged by knowing other Christians were praying for him. Is there some way you could let these Christians know you are doing the same?

3 NOT MY HOPE BUT HIS

Are you a fan of sporting events? Do you ever choose to watch sport on TV? Whilst there are moments of triumph, it often seems that being a fan of pretty much any sport involves a lot of hoping and not much fulfilment!

Read Philippians 1:6

Hope was something Paul had a lot of. However, fortunately for Paul, it wasn't the kind of vain hope experienced by most sporting followers, nor was it something he deliberately manufactured in an attempt to keep himself going. Paul's hope was built on something certain and he could be confident that it would one day bear fruit. Paul's hope differed from that of a sports fan in that it wasn't built on a trust in himself or even in the rest of humanity but on God's presence and power which sustained him in every situation.

God himself is our hope. We don't earn that hope; it is a gift given freely to all those who know God for themselves.

Spend some extra time with the giver of our hope. Be still in God's presence, perhaps reflecting on the words of Philippians 1:6. What do these words mean for you today?

3 How to build great relationships

Sadly, being a follower of Jesus doesn't guarantee that we are going to have great relationships with our fellow Christians. Some of the things we do will build those relationships but pretty often they'll undermine them. Fortunately, we aren't left to make our best guess about the most successful way to live. In Jesus we see a life lived well, the perfect model for us to follow.

Setting Out

Liking fish and chips, supporting a football team and drinking warm beer are all supposedly characteristics of the British. When people come to Britain they may choose to go through the process of becoming a British citizen but they aren't compelled to take on these supposed behavioural characteristics as well; nobody checks they're following the local team's results in the paper!

If you were asked to choose five kinds of behaviour that could be seen as traditional characteristics of people from your country, what would they be?

How many of the suggestions are true of you?

Do you think a person's nationality affects the kind of person they are or not?

Signposts

HEAVENLY CITIZENSHIP

Read Philippians 1:27–30
In the New Living Translation v 27 says, '. . . you must **live . . . as citizens of heaven**' conducting yourselves in a manner worthy of the good news about Christ. The Philippians were proud of being good citizens of a Roman city and Paul reminds them that they need to be more than good citizens of Philippi and of Rome; they should also be good citizens of heaven.

Unlike national citizenship, heavenly citizenship requires more than acquiring the right documents. Every citizen of heaven should acquire a new identity, a change meant to be visible in the way they live. As Paul put it, we should now live in a 'manner worthy' of the gospel.

As heavenly citizens, that new identity should affect our relationships.

Read Philippians 2:1–4

The quality of our relationships within the church itself is a vital element in our ability to share God's good news effectively with those outside.

There are three things that need to mark our relationships within God's community.

1 BEING OF ONE MIND AND PURPOSE

Paul calls us to agree wholeheartedly, love one another and work together with one mind and purpose. It's a lovely picture, isn't it, but does Paul think we should always agree on everything?

What if we just don't and can't agree on something? When should we speak out and when keep quiet?

What if speaking out changes nothing, what do we do then?

What does it mean for us as the members of a church to have one mind and purpose?

It's one thing for members of a single church to seek to have one mind and purpose but what about our relationships with those in different denominations? Is it possible that despite our many disagreements we could also be one in mind and purpose with them too?

If so, how might that be reflected in the way we approach our inevitable disagreements?

2 AVOIDING SELFISHNESS

Given a free choice, which one of each of these pairs of alternatives would you choose:

- too cold or too hot;
- walk or drive;
- tea or coffee;
- pews or chairs;
- World Cup or Wimbledon?

Did everybody agree with you on everything? Why was that?

We all like to have our own way but often our needs and desires come into conflict with those of others; we want one thing, they want something completely different. 'Don't be selfish. . .' says Paul. Selfish attitudes aren't unique to Philippi. In most churches there'll be someone who doesn't like the music, someone else who doesn't like the decor, another person who thinks something's being done all wrong. We don't have to agree about everything, but sometimes people fight their corner so hard that they miss the bigger picture. It can't always be about what suits me but what suits God's plans and purposes.

How does Paul say a person can learn to put aside their natural tendency to selfishness?

Paul talks about being humble. Does that mean we treat everyone's ideas as better than ours even if they're obviously ridiculous? Do we all go round saying 'after you' or 'it was nothing'? If not, what does he mean?

Paul doesn't want us to waste time and energy fighting amongst ourselves. It isn't just that we're spending time on the wrong things, but that our relationships are a part of our gospel message too. When they are wrong our message is undermined, when we get it right they help to demonstrate just what it really means to live God's way.

3 GIVING UP OUR RIGHTS

The internet is a great place to find out what people think. These are some things that people see 'as their right'. Do you agree with them?

- I will be as vocal about my opinions as I choose to be because it's my right.
- It's my right to work.
- It's my right not to smoke just as it should be to smoke.
- It's my money (paid as tax) and it's my right to know what they're doing with it.
- It's my right to do what I want with my body.
- If you hurt me, it's my right to sue you.

People use rights to justify behaviour. Sometimes that's legitimate but not always. As Christians we still do it. I can do this because . . . it's my right to be happy, my right to have what I want, my right to spend my money, my time and my energy as I please.

Do you think this is true of you? If so, when are you most likely to try to justify your behaviour in this way?

Paul and the Philippians demonstrate the need for all these three elements to be present in good relationships. However, sometimes the Philippian church is better at teaching us how not to do relationships instead! Paul goes on to remind them, and us, that instead of wondering how we should live, in Jesus we have an example we can follow without reservation.

BEING LIKE JESUS

Even when people come from the same community there can be a great deal of disagreement about the best way to live. Sometimes people are recommended to us as role models, people who it's worth trying to copy. A 2008 poll by Opinium Research asked British parents who they thought were good role models for their children. As well as Jesus, their responses included several well-known figures such as Richard Branson, Nelson Mandela, Jamie Oliver and Diana, Princess of Wales.

What do you think of those choices?

Who, apart from Jesus, would you have chosen and why?

As heavenly citizens, we have many great role models to follow but there can be no argument about who we should most want to be like. In the parents' poll he came third, but for us Jesus is always number one!

Paul reminds us of Jesus' attitude to his rights.

Read Philippians 2:5–11

In our world we are so often measured by what we can do, who we know, the influence we have over others, the status given by our position. Do we sometimes cling onto that power or position, even in church? Why does that happen?

Think about it in yourself.

- Have you ever carried on doing a job you were fed up with or no good at because it gave you a sense of value or importance you didn't want to lose? Are you doing it now?
- How do the things people do or don't do affect how you view them? Do you allow these attitudes to affect how you value them? Do you forget to value them just for who they are in God's eyes? Are you doing it now?

OBEDIENCE OVER RIGHTS

In many life situations pride and wrong values get in the way. As heavenly citizens we have a new model of behaviour. If anybody has the right to demand honour, glory and his own way in everything, it is Jesus, and yet he put obedience first. Jesus created the world, sustains life and still gave up all the benefits of his power and position for us.

Jesus wasn't forced to do what God wanted him to do; he could easily have chosen not to. Obeying God didn't lead Jesus into a comfortable place. Did he deserve the suffering that obedience brought him?

Why did he choose to obey him despite the immense personal cost?

For Jesus obedience was more important than holding onto what was fair or what he deserved; God's plans came first.

Have you ever thought 'it's not fair' when following Jesus made life difficult?

Have you ever wondered if making a different choice would have brought a different life – one with more money or a nicer place to live or more time for yourself?

Maybe we sometimes think if we hadn't followed Jesus we would still be friends with that person or we'd feel able to be rude to that irritating colleague instead of trying to learn to love them. If you've experienced these things, how did they make you feel?

Sometimes we may respond to these experiences by being resentful or angry or just fed up. Letting go of these feelings may be hard, perhaps we like to hold onto them and chew on them from time to time, maybe even try to impress others with our sacrifices. How could someone begin to let go of these difficult feelings?

Paul reminds us that obedience is the measure of success in God's eyes. For Jesus, obedience means that at his name one day every knee will bow and confess that he is Lord. We aren't promised that following Jesus will be an easy ride, but only that it will be worth it in the end.

Prayer

Read these verses in bold below, then the thoughts following it. Pause where marked for silent reflection.

Choose someone to read the verses and thoughts aloud to the group, allowing time for people to reflect at the marked points.

You must have the same attitude that Christ Jesus had.

How much do I want to be like Jesus? Is this my top priority or is something else more important to me? [pause]

Though he was God, he did not think of equality with God as something to cling to. Instead, he gave up his divine privileges he took the humble position of a slave and was born as a human being.

What do I cling to? What makes me feel valued by other people? [pause]

Could I let it go if God asked me to? How would I feel if I did? [pause]

When he appeared in human form, he humbled himself in obedience to God and died a criminal's death on a cross.

Has following Jesus been a good thing? Give thanks for God's blessings in your life. [pause]

However, obedience might ask a lot of me too. Do I want to serve God whatever the cost? [pause]

Therefore, God elevated him to the place of highest honour and gave him the name above all other names, that at the name of Jesus every knee should bow, in heaven and on earth and under the earth, and every tongue confess that Jesus Christ is Lord, to the glory of God the Father.

Jesus is Lord. May you truly be the Lord of my life today and every day. [pause and end]

Further Afield

1 FACING OPPOSITION

Read Philippians 1:27–29

Paul warns that as citizens of heaven we will face opposition. His words here are reminiscent of a speech given in the face of war. Paul speaks of 'standing side by side', 'fighting', not being 'intimidated', destruction and being saved, suffering and struggle.

Young people don't enter the Forces ready to go into battle straight away. How do they prepare?

Our way of battle is very different from a modern army, however. In 2 Corinthians 10:3–5 Paul says, 'We are human, but we don't wage war as humans do. We use God's mighty weapons, not worldly weapons, to knock down the strongholds of human reasoning and to destroy false arguments. We destroy every proud obstacle that keeps people from knowing God. We capture their rebellious thoughts and teach them to obey Christ.' (You may also like to look at Luke 6:27–36.)

So what or who are we fighting against?

Usually a war has an obvious end point; the enemy capitulates, the town is overrun, one side gains power over the other. What would it mean for us to win our war?

A key element of winning a war is good preparation.

Read Ephesians 6:13–18

How can we prepare for battle?

Are you ready? If not, what do you need to do?

You may like to ask God what you still need to do to prepare for battle.

If you feel you are facing a situation like this now bring that to God. You may also like to find someone else who can pray for you and support you through this time.

2 SUFFERING IS A PRIVILEGE

When you were at school, did some pupils have privileges that others didn't get?

How were you meant to feel when you finally qualified for these privileges?

A privilege suggests it's something good that we are glad to receive. Given a choice, would you prefer to suffer or not?

Paul says suffering is a privilege (Philippians 1:29) something presumably that we don't just have to endure bravely but can appreciate as bringing good things!

Read James 1:2–4

What can suffering develop in us?

Can we waste the experience of suffering?

Suffering tests and matures our faith, helping us to become more like Jesus. We don't have to enjoy it though. Job (Job 17:1), David (Psalms 38:8), Jesus (Matthew 26:38) and Paul himself (2 Corinthians 1:8) all speak of being 'crushed' to the point of being forced to rely utterly on God for their survival. Paul reminds us that suffering has a purpose and we should learn what we can from it.

3 AVENGING OURSELVES

Have you ever heard it suggested that if someone hurts you, you should hurt them in return? It can be a common attitude in the playground, but perhaps we sometimes like to carry it on into adult life too.

Have you ever tried to do this to someone, or have you had it done to you?

Read Luke 6:27–29

How should we respond to those who harm us?

Have you ever tried to love an enemy? How did it work out?

Read Romans 12:19–21

Whose responsibility is it to avenge evil?

Why do you think God doesn't want to leave vengeance to us?

What if God doesn't seem to do anything about the harm we've experienced? Why might that be? How should we respond then?

Jesus tells us to pray for the happiness of those who hurt us, perhaps one of the hardest things he calls us to do. Is there someone you need to pray for? If you find that impossible, tell him so and pray that he will help you want to pray for them.

4 *Light up the World*

*D*o you like the dark? Many of us as children will have demanded nightlights in our rooms or lights left on in the hall, maybe even refused to go upstairs alone. The dark can seem a dangerous place to be. However, even as we grow up and maybe lose some of those fears of bogey men and dragons hiding in the cupboard, the dark can remain pretty inconvenient at times. It makes it hard to see clearly, to find what we are looking for or where we are going. In a similar way Jesus describes people who live without him as 'stumbling through the darkness' (John 8:12), unable to see the way to real life. However, there is hope for them, and that hope is us, God's people. We are called to live lives that light up the world. We are to show people what it means to follow Jesus; to show them God's kingdom at work here on earth and to be the light showing the way to the giver of life himself.

Setting Out

Around the world few big celebrations from the launch of a sports event to New Year take place without a firework display. Think back to your childhood. What memories do you have of firework displays? What did you enjoy about them?

Were there certain types of firework you liked best? Why was that?

For many of us growing older sees the excitement of fireworks waning. How do you feel about firework displays today? Do you choose to buy or watch fireworks yourself?

In some countries it's quite hard for individuals to buy fireworks. They are perhaps only on sale for a very short time before they are needed. In other places there are few restrictions at all.

Which would you prefer to be the policy in this country? Would it be better to ban firework purchases by individuals altogether?

Signposts

Read Colossians 4:7–14 and Philemon 1:23–24

Paul probably wrote Colossians and Philemon about AD 60, slightly before his letter to the Philippians. What marked out the people Paul names in these verses?

Read 2 Timothy 4:10

2 Timothy was Paul's last letter, written around AD 65 or 66. What has happened to Demas in those few years since Paul wrote the earlier letters?

Demas wasn't someone who was just dabbling with following Jesus; he was so committed that he had been mentioned as one of Paul's key colleagues. Why do you think Demas let his commitment to serving God fall away?

Does his falling away mean his faith wasn't ever real after all?

What else might lead someone to let their faith grow cold?

Have you known people this happened to? Maybe it has happened to you at one time. What lay behind that?

Fireworks can make a big impact and be seen for many miles but they don't last for long. Jesus himself warned that the 'love of many' would grow cold (Matthew 24:12). We can be like fireworks with a faith that burns brightly but only lasts for a short time, or we can seek to live another way.

Read Philippians 2:12–18

Paul's words here encourage the Philippians not to give up but to keep on going; to persevere with their walk with God. Paul doesn't want their faith to fade into history, to be a short-lived 'firework' faith. In the New International Version, verse 15 encourages the Philippians to be like something that, rather than lasting for a few moments, lasts for billions of years. Paul calls them to live lives that 'shine like stars in the universe'. We are to seek a faith that endures, to live lives that go on lighting up the world with Jesus, day after day after day.

HOW TO BE A STAR (AND NOT A FIREWORK)

1 GET OUT THE POLISH (2:14)

Have you ever cleaned a window and then been stunned by how much clearer the view through it has suddenly become? Or cleaned your glasses and found the world doesn't have blurry splodges all over it after all?

Those windows, and our glasses, still kind of worked even though they were dirty. The marks didn't stop the light altogether; things just weren't as clear as they could have been. In just the same way wrong things, the dirty splodges of our lives, make it harder for other people to see God's light shining clearly in us. Paul gives us an example of those splodges when he talks about complaining and arguing. How does us behaving like this affect the way other people see God?

When we glance up at the sky it's the bright, shiny stars we pick out most easily. Paul encourages us to live lives where God is easily seen, to shine brightly. Arguing and complaining may be things we do recreationally or they may be completely alien. Whichever it is, there are things in everybody's life that make it harder for God to be seen in us. What are those things in you?

When we want to see through a dirty window or a pair of glasses we need to find a cloth and some cleaning fluid and use them to make a difference. In the same way, for God's light to shine brightly in our lives, we need to remove the splodges that stop that from happening. How do you think we could begin to do that?

2 TAKE ON THE FAMILY LIKENESS (2:15)

Have you ever made a phone call to someone, even someone you know really well, and found yourself confusing the voices of parent and child?

Family members can look alike, sound alike and even behave alike and it isn't always a genetic thing; it can be true for those brought up by adoptive parents or for husbands and wives too. Research has suggested that the longer people live together, the more likely they are to end up looking pretty similar to one another (a scary thought maybe!).

Do you think that you look like members of your family?

Or behave like them?

In his letter to the Philippians Paul speaks of being a slave of God and a citizen of heaven. Here he uses another picture to describe our relationship with God – being his child. The idea of the parent–child relationship suggests a much deeper personal connection than these other two pictures. When we live as a child in a family that makes a big impact on us; can you think of attitudes or practices that you picked up in childhood from your family and still demonstrate today?

Everyone's childhood experiences are different, some much more positive than others, and it may be that we are very glad not to be like members of our original family. However, as Christians, we are called to take on a new family likeness, to be like our perfect Father. What characteristics do you think that means we should take on?

How could that family likeness become more visible in us?

3 HOLD TIGHTLY TO THE WORD OF LIFE (2:16)

Have you ever been travelling and taken your passport and tickets around with you? How did you make sure you didn't lose them? Or did you mess up that task?

When something is really important we usually like to keep it close to us. Here Paul says 'hold tightly' to the word of life. He doesn't mean we must spend every minute of every day glued to our giant-print study Bible, though.

Read Hebrews 4:12

Hebrews 4:12

'For the word of God is full of living power. It is sharper than the sharpest knife, cutting deep into our innermost thoughts and desires. It exposes us for what we really are.'

Have you ever read a book, apart from the Bible, that really made a deep impact on you in some way?

Why not share these books with one another? What was it about it that made such an impression on you?

Perhaps sometimes when we read the Bible, we're interested to see what it says, we may learn something about life in Old Testament times or something about Paul's experiences, for example. However, perhaps we don't always read it expecting those words to make a difference to us, to the way we live our lives in the 21st century, and yet the author of Hebrews, whoever that was, says that God's Word is 'sharper than the sharpest knife'. What does he mean by that?

How is the Bible, God's Word, a source of life for us?

What does it really mean to hold tightly to it?

Read 1 John 1:1

The Word of Life is more than a thing, the Bible; it is a person, Jesus. To be changed we need not just to read the Bible, it's not enough to understand it or know a lot about it. For it to bring us life we need to know Jesus himself and become like him. The words contained in our Bibles are a means to life because they are a means to knowing Jesus better (see also John 5:39,40).

What do you think it means to hold tightly to Jesus?

We all hold tightly to something.

Spend a few moments considering what that might be in your life. Be honest. Do you really hold tightly to the Word of Life or does something else take precedence? Why is that?

What difference do you think it should make to someone's life if they are truly holding tightly onto Jesus?

FINALLY, BE THE REAL THING

Read Philippians 2:19–30

Timothy didn't have a firework faith; he didn't flare up brightly and then fade. Here Paul says, 'Timothy has proved himself'. In *The Message* those words are translated, 'Timothy's the real thing'. Over time, Timothy's way of living and his obedience to God have proved his faith to be true. Can we say with Timothy that our faith is 'the real thing', tested and true?

If we find that a hard question to answer, we can read Philippians 2:13 (NLT) and remind ourselves that it is God who transforms, 'all' we have to do is continue to obey him: 'For God is working in you, giving you the desire to obey him and the power to do what pleases him.'

Prayer

If it's a clear night and there's not too much light pollution around you might like to go outside and look up at the stars for a few moments. If not, be still and imagine that clear sky filled with stars.
Those stars, too many to count, show us that creation stretches far beyond our own earth. They give us a glimpse of the greatness of our creator God.
Give thanks for the vast majesty of God and his creation. You might like to use the words of Psalm 8 or another psalm that speaks about creation to begin your prayers.

Now imagine the followers of Jesus across the earth. We too are called to shine like the stars, to show others that there is something beyond the routines of daily life, to give them a 'glimpse of good living and of the living God' (from Philippians 2:15, *The Message*).

Pray that our lives, as individuals and as a church together might offer that glimpse of God to others.

Further Afield

1 RELATIONSHIPS MATTER

Read Philippians 2:19–24

Sometimes magazines and newspapers interview someone and ask them about the best teacher they ever had. Most people can remember a teacher who really made a difference in some way, someone whose enthusiasm for their subject or concern for them as a person inspired and encouraged them. Who was your best-ever teacher?

In some ways Paul and Timothy's relationship has been that of teacher and student as Paul has invested his time and energy in training and guiding Timothy. However, their relationship has become even more than that. Now it is like father and son, a closeness and depth of relationship that has transformed Timothy's life and borne fruit in his increasing spiritual maturity. Maybe you've not found someone quite that close but are there people who have invested time and energy in your life to help you mature as a Christian and a servant of Jesus?

Give thanks for those who have helped you mature in your faith and service. Pray that God would show you how you could encourage someone else in turn.

2 START NOTICING

Imagine someone you know well has changed their hairstyle, started wearing glasses or shaved off their beard. Would you

- be completely oblivious to the changes, even when they're pointed out to you;
- notice something was different but be uncertain just what it was;
- notice exactly what had changed down to the last details of colour and style?

Some of us are good at noticing details and some are just not! Have you ever found yourself in trouble for missing changes like these in someone else?

Why do you think people usually like these changes to be noticed by others?

Read Philippians 2:25–30

Whether Paul was good at spotting changes in people's appearance we don't know, but he was certainly good at spotting how people were serving Jesus. Epaphroditus has risked his life to serve Christ and Paul has not just noticed that but is now commending him for it to the Philippians. '. . . honour people like him,' he says.

Often our churches have people who perhaps don't have to risk their lives to serve, but through difficulties and challenges still go on serving faithfully without reward or even expecting thanks.

Who do you know like that? Perhaps this week you could encourage them by telling them how much you appreciate them, or sending them an email or even a card. We are called to serve for God to see, not for other people to honour us. Even so, that doesn't mean it isn't nice to get the odd thank you or other gestures of appreciation from time to time; a reminder that our work does not always go unnoticed.

3 WHO ARE YOU WHEN NO ONE'S WATCHING?

Read Philippians 2:12, 13

Imagine you're driving down a fairly empty motorway when suddenly everyone around you starts slowing down and driving much more sedately. As you keep going a distinctively marked car comes into view and you understand why those zooming along in the fast lane only a moment before have now decided to drive at a speed that exactly coincides with the speed limit.

When the representatives of the law are around, people seem much more careful to obey that law, don't they? Maybe that's true for you too. However, it doesn't necessarily just apply to the presence, or not, of the police does it? A class is likely to behave better in the presence of the teacher than when that teacher just nips out for a moment. When the boss is away, the office might just be little more relaxed about timekeeping. When the parents go away, the teenagers might just decide to invite a few friends over . . .

When Paul was with the Philippians, they diligently followed his lead, but now he isn't there any more. They have to go it alone and maybe that's the true test of their commitment to Christ. When nobody is watching, how do they behave then?

What about you, how do you behave when you aren't around other Christians?

Do you allow wrong actions to creep in because you think nobody is noticing?

God calls us to live lives that honour him whether anybody is noticing or not. Spend a few minutes thinking about the way you are around other Christians and then in other environments. Ask God to point out anything that slips when you are unobserved and resolve to change that with his help.

5 The gift of grace

*T*here was a time when many people believed that the world was flat. They would have defended that theory passionately and yet, as we now know, they were completely wrong. Have you ever believed something to be true and then discovered you were wrong?

Paul had that experience. He spent much of his life convinced he knew exactly how to be successful in God's eyes and how to live life God's way, only to discover one day that he had got it utterly upside down! Up to that point in his life he had been investing his time and energy in all the wrong things and his whole approach had to change. As Christians we can be passionate in our desire to serve God, but like Paul, find we have been wasting our time and energy on pursuing the wrong things.

Setting Out

Imagine you're wandering around the supermarket doing your shopping when you see a different brand of tea from your usual one is giving away a rather nice mug with each pack. Would you consider changing brands temporarily in order to get the freebie? (If you'd hate a mug but like a big bar of chocolate or a tea strainer that's fine – you get the idea, though.)

Do you like getting freebies with your shopping?

It's not just big chains that tempt us with free gifts. Magazines and newspapers can be other fruitful sources and you may well be able to think of others. What's the last thing you bought that came with a free gift of some kind (whether you went out of your way to get it or not)?

Shops don't just offer free gifts, many also have loyalty cards. How many do you have? Do you use them? Do you think the rewards make the cards worth having or not?

What's the best loyalty reward or free gift you've ever received?

Signpost

As a society we like to know what people do, it's often one of the first questions asked when people meet for the first time. Why is that do you think?

What do you think your immediate boss or the organisation that you work for value about their employees? Is it just what people achieve for them that matters? Should those we work for be concerned about anything else? (If you're not currently in paid employment you might like to think about a voluntary organisation you're part of, a job you held in the past, or even your schooldays.)

It's not just other people: friends, acquaintances or employers may measure someone's significance by what they do. Often we do it to ourselves as well. A significant percentage of the recently retired suffer from depression, in part because their sense of who they are and their significance in the world has been so closely bound up with their work.

How much of your self-esteem and sense of value is (or was) tied up in your work (or work you do for other groups, including church)?

If you were asked to define your purpose in life would your answer revolve around that work or not?

If that's not true for you, have there been times in the past when it would have been? If so, what changed?

FINDING VALUE

In our culture it so often seems that if we want to feel valued we must earn that right through doing useful things. Such attitudes seem to be hard-wired into many people and there's a danger that they affect our view of what it means to be a Christian as well.

Read Philippians 3:1–9

The good news of Jesus, of course, turns on the truth that what he has done for us is available to everyone as the ultimate free gift and here Paul discusses two big problems that people have with accepting this truth.

THE FIRST PROBLEM

We believe we gain God's favour when we do something to deserve it (3:2)

The idea that what you do affects how you are seen by others isn't a modern one. Here Paul finds it in and around the early church, seeping into the way people viewed their relationship with God. Even key people in the church struggled with this idea. You might like to read Paul's description of Peter's visit to Antioch, described in Galatians 2:11–16.

In Philippi these attitudes reflected wrong ideas about circumcision. Abraham's relationship with God depended on his faith, and he was then circumcised as a symbol of that faith. In Philippi people saw circumcision not as a symbol of inner faith but as something essential that they had to do before they could be right with God. If they didn't do it, God wouldn't accept them.

Paul is furiously angry with these people isn't he! Dogs, mutilators. . . he doesn't mince his words. Why does Paul get so worked up about them?

These people were talking about just one aspect of Jewish law but in the end what they were trying to do was earn God's favour. Such attitudes aren't lost in the mists of time; they are prevalent in the church today. We see ourselves as being accepted by God when we do things for him. We think to ourselves that God loves us more when we take on another church task, pray for an hour a day and go to our small group regularly and less when we turn the job down, forget to pray at all and skip the group this week.

Do you see this attitude in you? Has it ever been part of your thinking? If so, what kind of things do you find yourself thinking will make God love you more?

Such attitudes even permeate the church. Have you ever come across extra rules that churches expect you to obey before they will consider you to be a real Christian?

Read Galatians 2:19–21

Demanding that a Christian is circumcised, attends particular meetings or does enough jobs in the church are all attempts to earn God's approval through the things we do. What does Paul say here about such attempts?

What was the worst Christmas or birthday present you've ever received?

What did you do with it?

Rotten gifts can often end up being passed on to someone else, hidden in a drawer or even thrown away with the wrapping paper. When we try to earn God's love and favour through the things we do, we have missed the point. Paul even suggests that in effect we have thrown away the free gift of Jesus. We're trying to do the Christian life in our own way and are doomed to failure.

THE SECOND PROBLEM

We have the wrong priorities (3:5–10).

Who do you think are the most famous people in our society?

Are these people most famous for their character or their activities?

In general, our world values what a person achieves over the kind of person they are. When scandals break out, it's often argued that a person's private life should be irrelevant; we should focus only on the things they achieve or have achieved. Do you think that's true?

Paul had an impressive list of religious qualifications. How good are yours? Give yourself one mark for each of the following:

For each church service you attended in the last week;
For each service you arrived at on time;
For each time you took a friend or another member of your family who doesn't normally go to church;
For each time you helped to set up for, or tidy up after, one of those services;
For being baptised;
For owning at least three different versions of the Bible;
For being able to read Hebrew or New Testament Greek;
For reading (and completing) a Christian book in the last month;
If you've ever been paid to work for a church in any role;
If you've ever been a church elder or on a PCC or church board;
If you've ever headed up a church ministry area;
If you've ever helped in the kitchen after a service or cleaned the church toilets;
And finally one for each of the Ten Commandments you can remember without looking them up first! (The list is found in Exodus 20:1–17)

How did you do?

How did you feel about assessing your 'religious qualifications' in this way?

Paul would come out at the top of any test of religious qualifications and yet how does he describe his attitude to them? (3:7,8)

Why did he once see them as important do you think?

Paul says he has discarded his qualifications as garbage, so that he might gain Jesus instead (3:8). How could they have stopped him from knowing Jesus?

In the past Paul had worked hard to build and maintain this impressive list of achievements. Being a Pharisee was no easy ride: it required wholehearted concentration and yet now they are things he sees as completely unimportant. Paul has learnt to rely on something else instead.

RELYING ON THE RIGHT THINGS

Read Philippians 3:9 and Galatians 2:20

Paul once hoped that his circumcision and his long list of religious qualifications would get him into God's good books. What do these two verses say he is relying on now?

Paul's values have changed. His past achievements, his family history, his hard work have all become worthless to him because only one thing now really matters and that is knowing Jesus.

Some might say this isn't fair. They work hard for God and it should make a difference to his love for them. Do you agree with them?

Why do you think God doesn't work this way?

Do you think your relationship with Jesus is more important to you than anything else?

Do you find it easier to do something for God or spend time alone with him?

How does your use of your time demonstrate what is most important to you at the moment?

SERVICE STILL MATTERS

Read James 1:22–25 and 1 Peter 2:16

Paul may have known that all his effort couldn't make God love or value him more, but that didn't mean he just sat around doing nothing with his time (in fact, he strongly criticises those who did just that, see 2 Thessalonians 3:6–12).

So, imagine someone refuses to serve God or obey him, saying they only need faith in Jesus to be saved.

Does God love this person?

What do you think he might want to say to them?

Why does our service still matter to God?

Our achievements do matter to God, but they must flow from a heart and a life that is committed to him, a life whose first priority is in knowing Jesus.

Prayer

Read these verses taken from Philippians 3:8–11 in bold below, then the thoughts following it. Pause where marked for silent reflection.

Choose someone to read the verses and thoughts aloud to the group, allowing time for people to reflect at the marked points. End by saying the final prayer aloud together.

Everything else is worthless when compared with the priceless gain of knowing Christ Jesus my Lord.

Is this true in my life? How much does knowing Jesus really matter to me? Is Jesus really a priceless gift I value above anything else in my life? [pause]

I have discarded everything else, counting it all as garbage, so that I may have Christ and become one with him. I no longer count on my own goodness or my ability to obey God's law, but I trust Christ to save me.

God doesn't love me more when I pray more. God doesn't love me more because I'm busy doing things for church. God doesn't even love me more than someone who doesn't pray or misses church regularly or who refuses to help with the tea rota.

Do I try to earn God's love through the things I do? [pause]

God's way of making us right with himself depends on faith. As a result, I can really know Christ and experience the mighty power that raised him from the dead. I can learn what it means to suffer with him, sharing in his death, so that, somehow, I can experience the resurrection from the dead!

All I need, all anyone needs, to be acceptable to God is to trust in the free gift of Jesus. He is the one who reaches out and takes those tiny glimmers of faith, building on them and bringing us new life.

What difference has this gift made to my life? [pause]

Do I take God's love for granted or am I willing to offer him my whole heart and life in service? [pause]

Lord, I thank you for the free gift of Jesus. Help me to honour that gift by trusting wholeheartedly in your grace and mercy, not in the things I do. Help me to honour that gift by serving you day by day that others might come to know you too.

Further Afield

1 KEEP RUNNING THE RACE

How do you feel when you have to do something you're not very good at?

What subject were you worst at, at school? Did you enjoy it?

Quite often when we are bad at something we don't much like doing it, we are uncomfortable with imperfection. However, as Christians we know there are areas of our lives when, no matter how hard we try, we're going to fail again. Maybe there is a sin we just can't overcome at the moment, an attitude or an action that mars our lives but we aren't yet strong enough to eradicate permanently. The danger is that we give up and just live with it.

Read Philippians 3:12–14
Even Paul wasn't perfect, there were times he became deeply frustrated with his sinful self and yet he didn't give up. Paul understood that Jesus was more

patient with him than he was with himself, so instead of giving up he just kept on running the race as best he could in Christ's strength, one day at a time.

Are there particular sins that stand out when you think about your imperfections?

Pray that Jesus would help you keep on persevering, keep on working in you to change you and set you free from their effects.

End by reading these words that remind us that with God, every day can be a new beginning.

'The unfailing love of the Lord never ends! By his mercies we have been kept from complete destruction. Great is his faithfulness; his mercies begin afresh each day. I say to myself, "The Lord is my inheritance; therefore, I will hope in him!"' (Lamentations 3:22–24, NLT)

2 STEP BY STEP

Think about some of the skills you've learnt over the years. Maybe you can drive, make a shirt or solve complicated equations in your head. Did you ever start learning a skill and then give up before you could do it properly? Why was that?

When we learn a skill we start with the basics. People don't usually learn to read by picking up a novel off a shelf and getting going, they have to learn to recognise each individual letter and the sound associated with it first. We don't learn how to do those complex equations before we can recognise the numbers and understand how to add them up. We build up step by step until eventually, if we don't give up, we've practised the beginning stages so much we can move onto more complicated things.

Read Philippians 3:16

In the same way a decision to follow Jesus doesn't produce a mature person who understands everything overnight. We have to learn how to follow Jesus, step by step, practising the things we do know and understand until God says we're ready to learn something new.

Here Paul says that one test of our readiness to move on is putting what we already know into practice. God is longing to teach us more about following him, but until we do what he's already asked us to do – admitted that failing, started to serve in that particular area, forgiven that person we fell out with – then he may well decide we're not ready to learn more.

Are there things God has taught you that you aren't yet putting into practice? Why not decide to start changing this today? If you've found this hard in the past, is there someone who can help you take that first step?

3 FREEDOM

As a child what did you think being an adult would be like?

Many children go through a stage of looking forward to the freedom of being an adult, to all that independence and the chance to do exactly as you please. There's nobody to tell you when to go to bed, or control what you eat or make you go to school and lots of money to spend exactly as you liked! It's a fantasy world isn't it, a one-sided view of adulthood that has rather missed the point.

Read Philippians 3:17–21

God's grace offers us, adult or child, freedom too, doesn't it? We don't have to earn his love and we don't have to wallow in guilt because we didn't pray today or snapped at someone. However, Paul says that some people have missed the point. They are trading on God's grace, thinking it gives them the freedom to please themselves; to live a me-centred life. The consequence of that, Paul says, is that these people face eternal destruction because really their God is not God but themselves, and they haven't really come under God's grace at all. Living a God-centred life means taking on heavenly citizenship with all its rights and responsibilities.

Give thanks for the freedom God's grace gives to us. Ask God to show you how he wants you to respond to that grace in your life.

6 *Staying the course*

We live in a troubled world. Wars, concerns about our relationships, finances, the environment, our health, even just dissatisfaction with our lot in life; there is much that puts paid to sleep and contentment. Some deal with these things by ignoring them, perhaps through deliberate ignorance of world affairs, perhaps through alcohol or drugs, maybe through doing all they can to keep their little part of the world safe and just hoping nothing will damage that. Inevitably, though, the ups and downs of life will break through and have an impact on the most comfortable and secure of lives. How do we cope then? Does Jesus have something different to offer, a way of life, a real and lasting peace that will bring hope in the face of any trouble?

Setting Out

If you could choose to sign up for lessons in absolutely anything – a skill, a school subject, a professional qualification, whatever – for free, what would you choose and why?

Imagine a friend of yours had chosen to learn a new skill. It doesn't really matter what; it could be the art of wilderness map reading, tying knots, a new language, cookery, whatever. However, it's a long time since they learnt a new skill and they come to you for your three top tips for success. What would you suggest they do to help themselves acquire this new skill?

1.

2.

3.

If you want to learn to speak Swahili, it's no good going to German lessons or even going to the right lessons but then spending all your time practising golf instead. We need to get the right information into our heads and then we need to put what we've learnt into practice before it has any chance of becoming second nature.

Why might someone start Swahili lessons but then not bother practising?

What skills have you learnt recently?

Did practising make a difference? How easy did you find it to put in the time?

Signposts

STAND FIRM

Read Philippians 4:1

Paul's plea to his beloved Philippians is that they should stay true; stand firm in the Lord. Why do you think he thought this was so important? What might happen if they didn't?

Every person faces difficulties in life, and following Jesus doesn't protect us from that but it can make a difference to the way we face them and their impact on us. For that to happen, Paul says we need to learn and then put into practice a skill that perhaps doesn't come too easily to most of us, the skill of living peacefwully.

There are four areas of life where we need to practise peace.

1 PEACE WITHIN THE CHURCH

Read Philippians 4:2, 3 and Luke 11:17

This disagreement between Euodia and Syntyche had obviously been going on for a while, long enough for Paul to have heard about it and include it in this letter. We might assume that when we fall out with someone in the church that it's a private thing, just between us and them but Paul obviously thought it important enough to raise in a public letter. Why do you think he didn't just send a second, private note to them both?

Anyone can fall out and refuse to repair the relationship, not everyone is willing to rebuild it. Why was it so important for them to sort out their problems with one another?

Paul asks his 'true teammate' to help them sort things out. Obviously not every falling out requires a third person to get involved. When do you think a third person should step in?

If someone is going to get involved, how should we choose that person? Is it just the first to volunteer?

Euodia and Syntyche were spending their energy on practising the art of falling out rather than the art of building good relationships with one another. In Ephesians 4:31, 32 (New Living Translation) Paul sums up the things we need to practise in our relationships saying, 'Get rid of all bitterness, rage, anger, harsh words, and slander, as well as all types of malicious behaviour. Instead, be kind to each other, tender-hearted, forgiving one another, just as God through Christ has forgiven you'.

Which of these things are you practising with those around you in your church?

Is there someone you need to forgive or with whom you need to repair your relationship? If so, what first step towards that could you take? Is it time to ask a third person to get involved or is it still possible for you to sort it out by yourselves?

How do you think having good relationships with one another will help us to stand firm in our faith; to stay true to Jesus?

2 PEACE WITH EVERYONE

There's just one parking space left at work and you're approaching it when you see an irritating colleague coming in the other direction. You're going to arrive fractionally before them. Do you

- wave cheerily at them as you drive into that space;
- slow down and wave cheerily as they take it (despite their smug expression)?

Your noisy neighbour moans that your child is kicking a ball against their wall and disturbing them. Do you

- get your child to stop (at least whilst the neighbour's in);
- get your child to play there with their friends as well?

Read Philippians 4:4, 5

Paul is not just interested in the Philippians' relationships with one another. 'Let everyone see that you are considerate in all you do', he says (4: 5). Why might it be important for us to get along with those outside the church too?

Relationships affect how people see us. If they know we go to church but their experience of us is that we are miserable and mean, then that's quite likely to end with them having a pretty negative view of church as well. Our message of good news isn't likely to be heard by someone who doesn't like us much!

Think about the way you relate to your neighbours, your colleagues or others around you who don't follow Jesus. Are any of them getting a very negative view of who you are and, perhaps more importantly, not being able to see Jesus in you?

What could you do to improve that relationship?

Sometimes people don't want to rebuild a damaged relationship. Within the church there is the potential to get a third person involved but that may not be possible with those outside it, our neighbours, for example. Is there anything we can do when the other person refuses to try to repair the damage?

Are there ever times we should just let a damaged relationship go, in or out of the church, and not try to mend it?

3 PEACE IN OURSELVES

Read Philippians 4:6, 7

You hear on the news that in 2017 there is a tiny possibility of an asteroid hitting the earth. Do you

- sign up to several asteroid tracking websites so you can keep an eye on it;
- make plans for your back garden underground survival cave and lists of supplies;,
- forget the information within 10 seconds of hearing it;
- remember it from time to time with a twinge of concern but do nothing about it . . . yet?

You hear at work that Mary's cousin's next door neighbour's son works with poultry and has contracted flu. She says 'they' think it just might be H5N1, 'Killer' Bird Flu. Do you

- start researching places you can buy your own vaccine;
- laugh at her for being so gullible;
- go and buy a chicken sandwich to show solidarity with the poultry workers;
- make soothing noises but watch the news rather closely for a few days?

You made a significant mistake at work today. Do you

- go home and forget about it;
- wake up in the middle of the night panicking and spend the rest of the night planning what to do as soon as you get in tomorrow;
- get home and then either go straight back again to sort it or ring your boss to discuss it;
- pretend you've got flu so you don't have to go in for a few days and hope it's all quickly forgotten?

Do you think that you are a worrier?

'In your life expect some trouble, but when you worry you make it double. Don't worry, be happy.' (Bobby McFerrin, 1988)

'Don't worry, be happy.' Is this good advice?

Is it possible to ignore every worry in life and just be happy?

When you are worried, what do you tend to do with those concerns?

What would Paul have suggested you did with your time?

For many of us being worried means either spending less time praying or at least praying in quick bursts rather than a time to slow down and spend more time with God. Paul doesn't suggest that prayer is the way to remove every problem in life but that it is the way to face them, that it can bring God's peace into our lives. In troubled times, God needs to be our first priority.

At the last supper Jesus said, 'I am leaving you with a gift – peace of mind and heart. And the peace I give isn't like the peace the world gives. So don't be troubled or afraid'. John 14:27. Peace in the world's eyes comes from getting rid of the problem or perhaps in thinking positively in the face of our ongoing troubles. However, Jesus says his peace is different. If his peace doesn't come from the ending of our troubles or through having happy thoughts, what is it based on?

Prayer, for Paul, didn't mean rehearsing the problem over and over again. What did he expect us to do during our prayer times?

Do you find it easy to let go of worried or panicky thoughts? Sometimes perhaps we start to pray with these thoughts in our heads and end with them still there, without any sense of God's peace and presence. What could you suggest to someone if that happens to them?

How can knowing God's peace help us to stay true to Jesus when life gets tough?

4 PEACE IN ALL CIRCUMSTANCES

Read Philippians 4:9–13

Do you think adverts encourage us to be content with our lives as they are?

Imagine you had a life filled with all the objects and holidays that you see in the adverts. Would that make you contented?

Instead of contentment someone may experience dissatisfaction and disappointment. Perhaps they're jealous, maybe they've failed to live up to their own hopes and dreams, or maybe they just don't feel they have enough. Whatever lies behind it, what they have now isn't what they wanted; it doesn't feel like life is the best it could be.

What kind of things might someone do to try and change those feelings of dissatisfaction with their lives?

Paul's life wasn't obviously going well but he wasn't dissatisfied. Do you think he was just someone who was naturally easily pleased?

Read Philippians 1:21 and 4:12, 13

Paul has learnt that if we focus on what we want or what we don't have, we will never be satisfied. Why is that?

What should we focus on instead?

Do you think that the call to contentment, whatever the circumstances, means that those who have very little in our society or around the world should just get on with it and never protest?

How might learning the art of being contented help us to stay true to Jesus in our world today?

What makes you discontented with your life at present?

Do you think you sometimes practise your discontentment by going over and over your disappointments in life?

Are you ready to put that aside and listen to what Jesus wants for you instead?

Are you ready to trust that he will 'supply all your needs' (Philippians 4:19)?

Are you ready to practise focussing on his priorities not your own?

Read Philippians 3:13, 14 and Philippians 4:9 one more time.

Paul was a great model for young churches and Christians to follow. He knew he wasn't the finished product but could show that he was doing his best to live a life that would honour Jesus right to the end, something that in putting his teaching into practice can be true for us too.

Think back over these sessions in Philippians. What is the most important message you will take away from reading this book?

Prayer

As God's community, God's light to the world, we need to demonstrate the art of living peacefully. In which of the areas above do you find it hard to be peaceful?

As a community of people who share the same purpose and desire to serve God, it is good to encourage one another as we try to live God's way. Pray for one another, that you might learn to know God's peace in the areas you find most difficult at the moment.

You might also like to pray for peace in:

- your church;
- your local community;
- the wider world.

End by praying for one another, perhaps following up on the things people will take away from reading this letter. You might like to pray this sentence for each person in turn.

Lord, we pray that [NAME] would put into practice these words of life. May their life shine with your light and your love, that through them others may have a glimpse of good living and of the living God.

Further Afield

1 SEEK THE GOOD

Think back over the past day or so. What has been filling your thoughts in that time?

Discard the practical things, the process of shopping and cooking tea or activities at work.

What else has been in your mind? Are these good things or not?

Read Philippians 4:8

Some things come into our heads because of what we choose to watch, to read, to look at on the internet or to talk about, although its not always easy to decide what isn't good for us.

For example, do you think there are some things on TV that don't promote Paul's list of good qualities? Do you watch some of these? If so, does it matter?

Do Paul's words mean that we shouldn't watch the news, or read thrillers and crime novels?

Do you think everything is equally harmful for every person or are some more affected than others, or is that just self-deception?

What do you think it means for us to fix our thoughts on things that are excellent and worthy of praise?

Be still before God. Be honest with yourself about the impact of things you do on your mind. Ask him to show you if there are things you need to stop doing in order to rid yourself of harmful influences.

2 BEING REWARDED

Do you do your job for the money or are there other rewards as well? Paul had two jobs for most of his Christian life; he was a tentmaker to bring in the money he needed to live, and God's apostle, something that brought him very different rewards.

Read Philippians 4:1
How does Paul describe the Philippians themselves?

What does Paul mean when he says the Philippians are his 'reward'?

What kind of rewards do we seek when we serve God?

- Do we seek the applause of others as the Pharisees did? (Matthew 6:5)
- Do we seek practical rewards?
- Are we content when our reward is the happiness or changed lives of others?
- Are we content with no obvious reward beyond God's approval?

Give thanks for the opportunities God gives you to serve him and others. Ask him to show you if sometimes you are doing it for the wrong motives, for tangible rewards, rather than for him alone.

3 BE JOYFUL

'Happiness is a cigar called Hamlet.' Do you remember that slogan, one of the most famous advertising slogans in the UK ever? However, if that was true, happiness was something that didn't last very long and wasn't available all the time. Perhaps that is true! Happiness is something we don't experience all the time. However, there is something often confused with happiness that Paul says we should be able to experience always, all day, every day.

Read Philippians 4:4

Joy seems an even deeper emotion than happiness. We perhaps assume joy is something we can experience only rarely and yet Paul was in prison and joyful at the same time.

Paul's joy came not from the things happening to him but from the certainty that he was in God's hands through the good times and the bad, that he never faced these things alone. In Romans 8:31 he says, 'If God be for us, who can be against us'. If we choose to put Jesus first in our lives, we will know God's power and love and joy in every situation.

Celebrate God today. Give thanks for his character, the things about him that are worthy of praise. Give him the pleasure of some extra time in your company. And whatever your circumstances, practise being joyful, sure that he is with you whatever happens.

About the Author

Kate Hayes became a Christian aged 12 after being 'dragged along' to a
Pathfinder meeting by a friend. After studying Psychology at university she did
teacher training but then changed direction, working in bookshops and in
software testing for the book trade. Since 1994 her family have been in
Dukinfield, Greater Manchester, where she co-ordinates and writes materials
for small groups at St John's Church.

OTHER TITLES by KATE HAYES

A Journey of the Heart: a pilgrim's guide to prayer

A companion to this book, with identical format. If you want to explore
what it means to pray with purpose, growing in understanding of and
intimacy with your God, this series of six Bible-based studies – which can
be tackled in a small group or on your own – will take you on a rewarding
journey. 48pp
ISBN 1 85999 797 X

The Journey of the Son

The second in this series of studies. Based on Matthew's portrayal of Jesus' road
to the cross, these six studies consider the struggles we also face to do God's
will. We see how Jesus coped with temptation and emotional turmoil, and stayed
the course to the end. 56pp
ISBN 1 84427 097 1

A Journey of Discovery: on the road with Jesus' followers

Kate Hayes invites us to dig deeper into Luke's portrayal of how the first
disciples grew in their understanding of Jesus and what it meant to be his
disciples. What should be our priorities as we seek to live God's way? How
can we cope with pressure and failure? 64pp
ISBN 1 84427 180 3

A Journey of Love: reaching out as Jesus did

Throughout his life Jesus was guided by a clear sense of mission. We too are
called to reach out in love as Jesus did. Kate Hayes invites us to think about
what it meant for Jesus to be sent by his Father and what it means for us to
follow Jesus' example today. 64pp
ISBN: 978 1 84427 232 7

The Journey to Wisdom
In this guide we explore the journey to wisdom we can all make – learning how to live wisely in terms of attitudes to success and goals in life, in our choices and decisions, our speech and relationships. Ultimately we see what wisdom is in Jesus going the way of the cross. 64pp
ISBN: 978 1 84427 285 3

All suitable for individual or group use, at Lent or any other time.

THE RE:ACTION SERIES – SMALL GROUP RESOURCE
For the tough times
Does God care when I'm hurting?
Whether it's thousands killed in a terrorist attack as you watch on TV, your next door neighbour on chemo for cancer, or your best friend's marriage on shaky ground . . . there's no escaping the issue of suffering. Maybe you want to shout at God that's it's just so unfair! Just what's it all for? 48pp
ISBN 1 85999 622 1

Available from all good Christian bookshops or from Scripture Union Mail Order: PO Box 5148, Milton Keynes MLO, MK2 2YX, tel: 0845 0706006 or online through www.scriptureunion.org.uk

SCRIPTURE UNION
USING THE BIBLE TO INSPIRE CHILDREN, YOUNG PEOPLE AND ADULTS TO KNOW GOD